T0413918

CAROLINA
PANTHERS

BY JOSH ANDERSON

Stride

An Imprint of The Child's World®

childsworld.com

The Child's World®
childsworld.com

Published by The Child's World®
800-599-READ • www.childsworld.com

Photography Credits

Cover: © Andy Lyons / Staff / Getty Images; page 1: © Africa Studio / Shutterstock; page 3: © Grant Halverson / Stringer / Getty Images; page 5: © Streeter Lecka / Staff / Getty Images; page 6: © Craig Jones / Staff / Getty Images; page 9: © Mike Ehrmann / Staff / Getty Images; page 10: © Streeter Lecka / Staff / Getty Images; page 11: © stevezmina1 / Getty Images; page 12: © Grant Halverson / Stringer / Getty Images; page 12: © Mike Comer / Stringer / Getty Images; page 13: © Grant Halverson / Stringer / Getty Images; page 13: © Streeter Lecka / Staff / Getty Images; page 14: © Jared C. Tilton / Staff / Getty Images; page 15: © Brian A. Westerholt / Stringer / Getty Images; page 16: © Jacob Kupferman / Stringer / Getty Images; page 16: © Michael Reaves / Stringer / Getty Images; page 17: © Streeter Lecka / Staff / Getty Images; page 17: © Streeter Lecka / Staff / Getty Images; page 18: © Andy Lyons / Staff / Getty Images; page 18: © Al Messerschmidt / Staff / Getty Images; page 19: © Dirk Shadd/ZUMAPRESS / Newscom; page 19: © Grant Halverson / Stringer / Getty Images; page 20: © Norm Hall / Stringer / Getty Images; page 20: © Grant Halverson / Stringer / Getty Images; page 21: © Grant Halverson / Stringer / Getty Images; page 21: © Grant Halverson / Stringer / Getty Images; page 22: © Streeter Lecka / Staff / Getty Images; page 23: © Nick Laham / Staff / Getty Images; page 23: © stevezmina1 / Getty Images; page 25: © Jamie Squire / Staff / Getty Images; page 26: © Norm Hall / Stringer / Getty Images; page 29: © Leon Halip / Stringer / Getty Images

ISBN Information
9781503857889 (Reinforced Library Binding)
9781503860421 (Portable Document Format)
9781503861787 (Online Multi-user eBook)
9781503863149 (Electronic Publication)

LCCN 2021952692

Printed in the United States of America

TABLE OF CONTENTS

GO PANTHERS!

The Carolina Panthers compete in the National Football **League's** (NFL's) National Football Conference (NFC). They play in the NFC South **division**, along with the Atlanta Falcons, New Orleans Saints, and Tampa Bay Buccaneers. Although the Panthers are the newest team in the NFC, fans have witnessed plenty of highlights from the team. They haven't won yet, but Carolina has made it to the **Super Bowl** twice in their short history. Let's learn more about the Panthers.

NFC SOUTH DIVISION

Atlanta Falcons

Carolina Panthers

New Orleans Saints

Tampa Bay Buccaneers

CHRISTIAN MCCAFFREY AND CAM NEWTON FORMED A FIERCE DUO ON OFFENSE FOR THE PANTHERS IN 2017 AND 2018.

BECOMING THE PANTHERS

The Panthers joined the league as an **expansion team** in 1995. The franchise is named after the Carolina panther, an animal that sadly is now extinct in the wild. The Panthers finished with a 7–9 record in their first season. That's the best record ever for an NFL expansion team. In their second season, the team won 12 games and came within one win of making it to the Super Bowl.

UNLIKE MOST EXPANSION TEAMS, THE PANTHERS WERE QUICK TO BE COMPETITIVE AGAINST THE NFL'S EXISTING TEAMS.

BY THE NUMBERS

The Panthers have played in **TWO** Super Bowls.

SIX division titles for the Panthers

500 points scored by the team in 2015— a team record!

15 wins for the Panthers in 2015

THE 2015 NFC CHAMPION CAROLINA PANTHERS SCORED MORE POINTS THAN ANY OTHER TEAM IN THE NFL THAT SEASON.

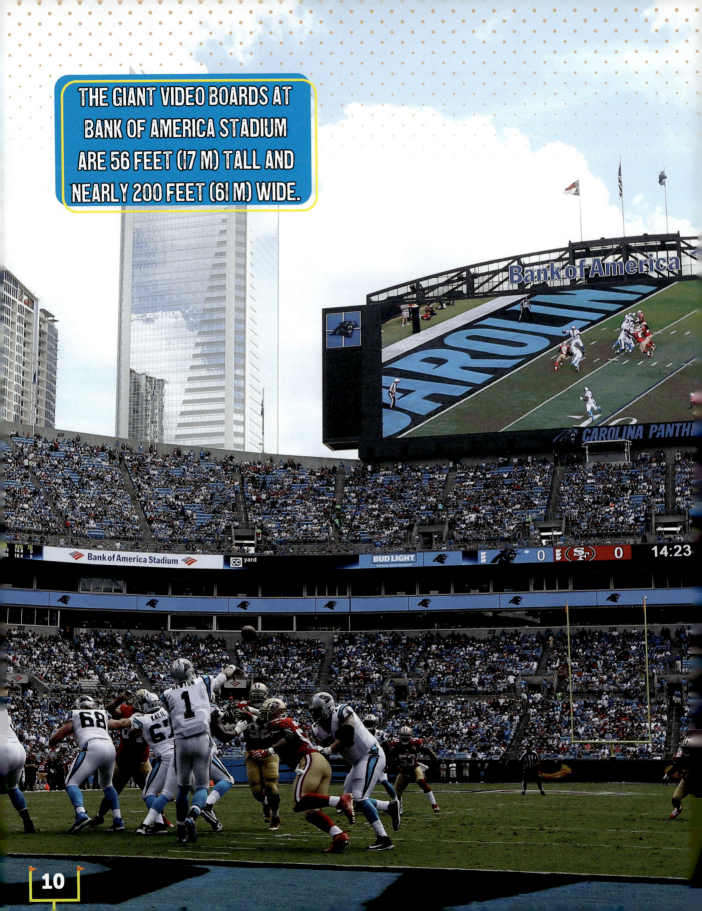

THE GIANT VIDEO BOARDS AT BANK OF AMERICA STADIUM ARE 56 FEET (17 M) TALL AND NEARLY 200 FEET (61 M) WIDE.

The Panthers played their first season at Clemson University's Memorial **Stadium**. Since then, the team has called Bank of America Stadium in Charlotte, North Carolina, its home. Many parts of the stadium incorporate the team's blue, silver, and black color scheme. Each one of the stadium's three entrances is "guarded" by two huge bronze panther sculptures. Bank of America Stadium can hold about 75,000 Panthers fans on game days.

We're Famous!

A 2017 episode of the ABC game show *$100,000 Pyramid* must've delighted Panthers fans. Quarterback Cam Newton competed on the program against another football star, New York Giants wide receiver Brandon Marshall. Each player was paired with a contestant and competed for two rounds. Newton managed to defeat Marshall in each round.

UNIFORM

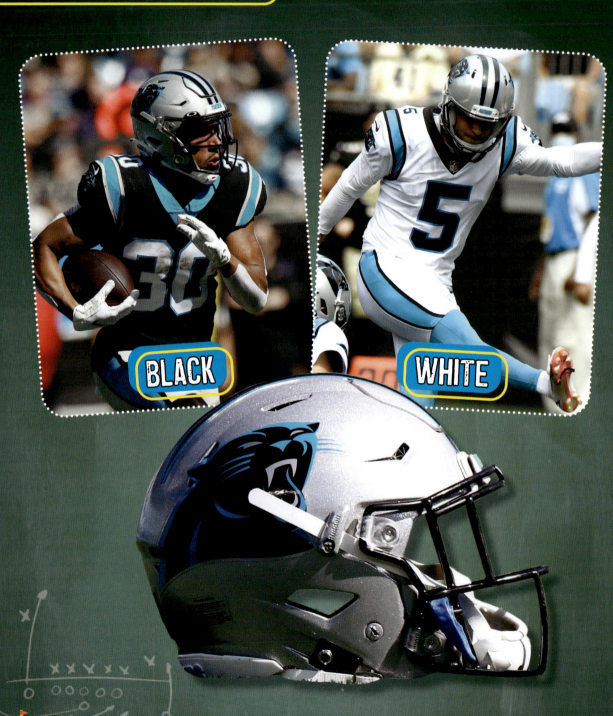

BLACK

WHITE

Truly Weird

Panthers mascot Sir Purr once tried to get in on the action during the game! During a 1996 game, the Pittsburgh Steelers punted the ball into the Panthers' end zone. Before a player from either team could touch the ball, Sir Purr pounced on the ball, forcing Carolina to settle for a touchback.

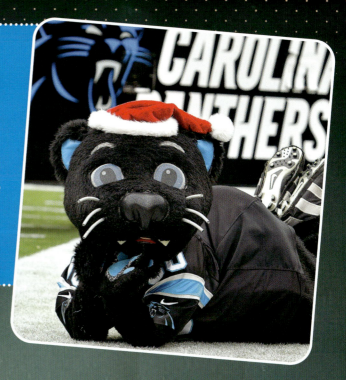

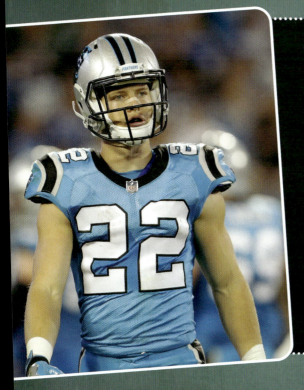

Alternate Jersey

Sometimes teams wear an alternate jersey that is different from their home and away jerseys. It might be a bright color or have a unique theme. The Panthers wore all-blue uniforms for a Thursday night game against the Philadelphia Eagles in 2017. The new look proved unlucky, though. The Panthers lost the game.

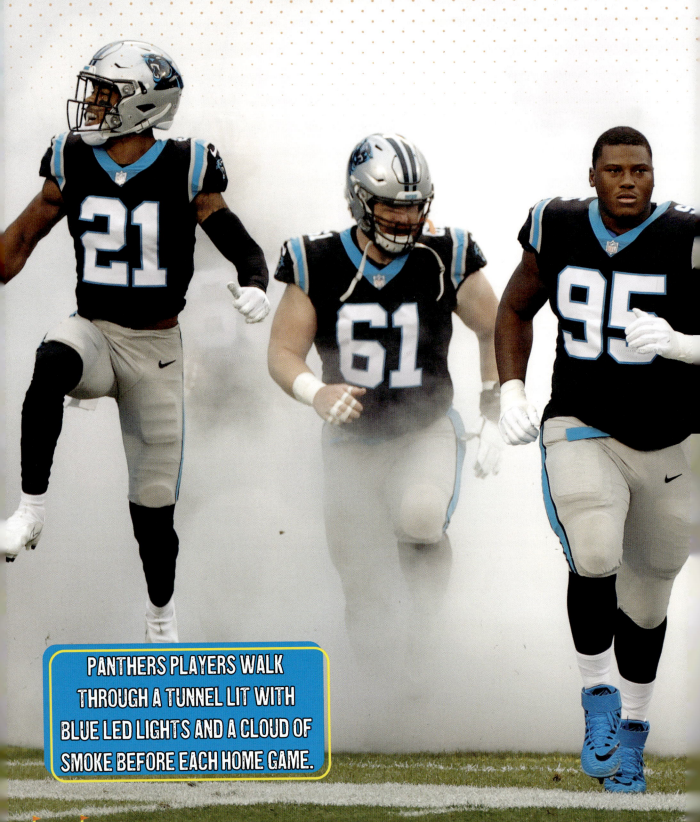

PANTHERS PLAYERS WALK THROUGH A TUNNEL LIT WITH BLUE LED LIGHTS AND A CLOUD OF SMOKE BEFORE EACH HOME GAME.

Going to a game at Bank of America Stadium can be tons of fun! Fans of the team scream "Keep Pounding" as a way to inspire the players on the field. After every Panthers win, fans sing the song "Sweet Caroline" as it plays throughout the stadium. The TopCats Cheerleaders entertain the crowd at every game. And joining the TopCats to get the crowd excited is Sir Purr, a costumed black panther. Hungry fans can find some truly unique food choices at the stadium. The Frito chili pie dog is a hot dog topped with chili, cheddar cheese, onions, jalapeños, and Fritos.

SIR PURR

Luke Kuechly
Linebacker | 2012–2019

Nicknamed "Captain America," Kuechly made the **Pro Bowl** every season of his career except his first. He led the league in combined tackles twice. Kuechly finished his career with 18 interceptions and started every one of the 118 games he played in the NFL.

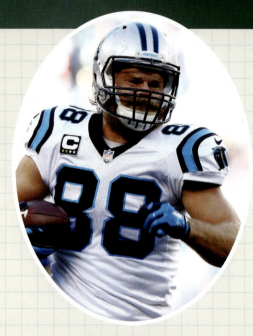

Greg Olsen
Tight End | 2011–2019

Olsen's 6,463 receiving yards are the third most in team history. Olsen also caught 39 **touchdowns** during his time in Carolina. He finished with more than 1,000 yards receiving three times. Olsen also was selected for the Pro Bowl three times.

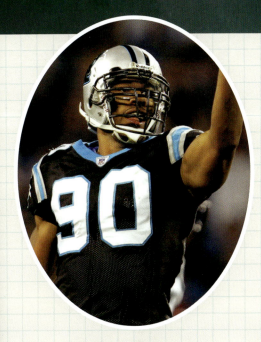

Julius Peppers
Defensive End | 2002–2009; 2017–2018

Peppers's 97 **sacks** are the most in team history. He ranks third in NFL history with 175 tackles for loss. Peppers was chosen for five Pro Bowls during his time in Carolina. He helped lead the Panthers to their first appearance in the Super Bowl.

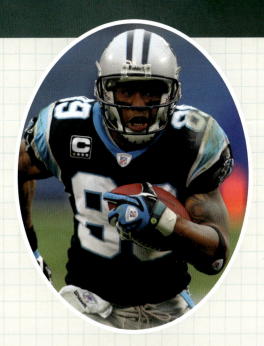

Steve Smith
Wide Receiver | 2001–2013

Smith ranks eighth all-time with 14,731 receiving yards. His 103 catches, 1,563 receiving yards, and 12 touchdowns in 2005 all led the NFL that season. He finished with more than 1,000 receiving yards seven times during his Panthers career. He was chosen for five Pro Bowls.

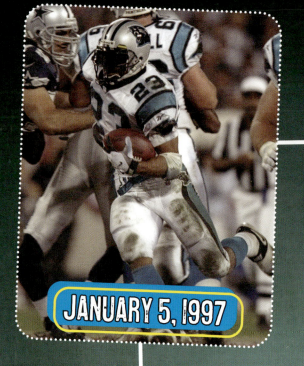

In only their second season in the league, the Panthers defeat the Dallas Cowboys 26–17 and advance to the NFC Championship Game.

JANUARY 5, 1997

The Panthers defeat the Bears 29–21 and earn another trip to the NFC Championship Game.

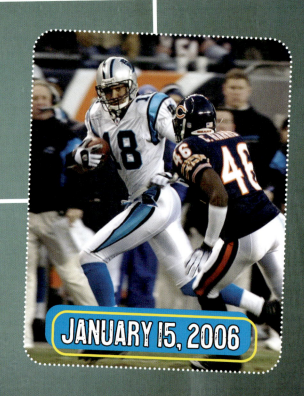

JANUARY 15, 2006

BIG DAYS

APRIL 28, 2011

With the first overall selection in the NFL Draft, the Panthers select quarterback Cam Newton from Auburn University.

The Panthers defeat the Arizona Cardinals in the NFC Championship Game and earn a trip to play in Super Bowl 50.

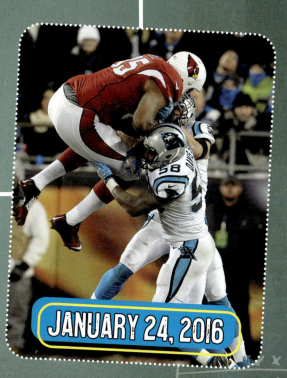

JANUARY 24, 2016

MODERN-DAY MARVELS

Brian Burns
Defensive End | Debut: 2019

After Burns starred at Florida State University, the Panthers chose him with their first-round pick in the 2019 NFL Draft. He totaled 25.5 sacks in his first three seasons and led the team with nine in 2020. He also led the team with three forced fumbles. Burns was selected for his first Pro Bowl appearance following the 2021 season.

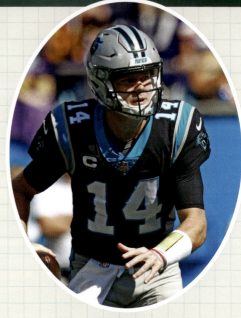

Sam Darnold
Quarterback | Debut: 2021

Darnold starred at the University of Southern California during his college career, throwing for 57 touchdowns over two seasons. Darnold joined the Panthers in 2021 after playing his first three seasons with the New York Jets. Darnold won his first three starts as a Panther. He rushed for five touchdowns in his first four games with Carolina.

Christian McCaffrey
Running Back | Debut: 2017

In 2018, McCaffrey became the first player ever with 50 rushing yards and 50 receiving yards in five-straight games. In 2019, he led the NFL with 2,392 total yards and 19 total touchdowns. His 116 catches in 2019 were the most ever by an NFL running back.

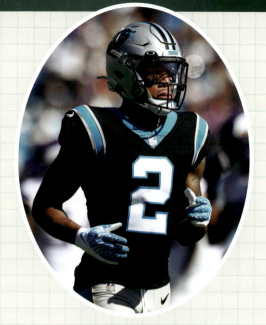

D. J. Moore
Wide Receiver | Debut: 2018

The Panthers selected Moore in the first round of the 2018 NFL Draft. He led all **rookie** wide receivers in 2018 with 960 total yards. Moore was the only receiver in the NFL with more than 1,200 total yards in 2019, 2020, and 2021.

CAM NEWTON'S SIGNATURE CELEBRATION IS TO ACT AS IF HE'S RIPPING OFF HIS JERSEY TO REVEAL A SUPERMAN LOGO UNDERNEATH.

CAM NEWTON

Newton led the Panthers to 68 regular season wins during his nine seasons with the team, from 2011 until 2019. He rejoined the team for eight games during the 2021 season. Newton led the team to a 15–1 record in 2015 and a trip to Super Bowl 50. He also led the team to the **playoffs** four times. He's the all-time leader in rushing touchdowns for a quarterback. Newton is the only player in NFL history to pass for 30,000 yards and rush for 5,000 yards.

FAN FAVORITE

Jake Delhomme–Quarterback
2003–2009

Delhomme will forever have a place in the hearts of Carolina fans after leading the team to its first Super Bowl after the 2003 season. He also led the team to 53 regular season victories. Delhomme ranks second in team history with 19,258 passing yards.

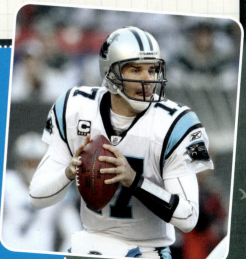

#1

THE BIG GAME

The Panthers had played in the NFC Championship Game once before but had yet to play in a Super Bowl. The Philadelphia Eagles had home field advantage and were favored to win the game against the Panthers and advance to Super Bowl 38. The Panthers took the lead in the second quarter on a touchdown pass from Jake Delhomme to Muhsin Muhammad. They would score again later, but that first touchdown was all they needed. Behind three interceptions from cornerback Ricky Manning, the Panthers held the Eagles to only a field goal and won the game 14–3. The Panthers were headed to their first Super Bowl.

DESHAUN FOSTER RAN FOR 60 YARDS AND SCORED A TOUCHDOWN IN THE PANTHERS' NFC CHAMPIONSHIP GAME WIN OVER THE EAGLES.

RON RIVERA'S 76 REGULAR SEASON VICTORIES ARE THE MOST FOR A COACH IN PANTHERS HISTORY.

AMAZING FEATS

4,436 Passing Yards

In 1999 by **QUARTERBACK** Steve Beuerlein

1,515 Rushing Yards

In 2008 by **RUNNING BACK** DeAngelo Williams

16 Receiving Touchdowns

In 2004 by **WIDE RECEIVER** Muhsin Muhammad

146 Points Scored

In 2015 by **KICKER** Graham Gano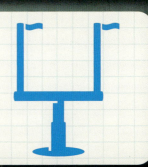

ALL-TIME BEST

PASSING YARDS

Cam Newton
29,725*

Jake Delhomme
19,258

Steve Beuerlein
12,690

RUSHING YARDS

Jonathan Stewart
7,318

DeAngelo Williams
6,846

Cam Newton
5,036*

RECEIVING YARDS

Steve Smith
12,197

Muhsin Muhammad
9,255

Greg Olsen
6,463

SACKS**

Julius Peppers
97

Charles Johnson
67.5

Mike Rucker
55.5

SCORING

John Kasay
1,482

Graham Gano
742

Steve Smith
454

INTERCEPTIONS

Chris Gamble
27

Eric Davis
25

Luke Kuechly
18

*as of 2021
**unofficial before 1982

JONATHAN STEWART RUSHED FOR 51 TOUCHDOWNS FOR THE TEAM FROM 2008 TO 2017.

GLOSSARY

division (dih-VIZSH-un): a group of teams within the NFL that play each other more frequently and compete for the best record

expansion team (eks-SPAN-shun TEEM): a new team added to the league

league (LEEG): an organization of sports teams that compete against each other

playoffs (PLAY-ahfs): a series of games played after the regular season that decides which two teams play in the Super Bowl

Pro Bowl (PRO BOWL): the NFL's All-Star game where the best players in the league compete

rookie (RUH-kee): a player playing in his first season

sack (SAK): when a quarterback is tackled behind the line of scrimmage before he can throw the ball

stadium (STAY-dee-uhm): a building with a field and seats for fans where teams play

Super Bowl (SOO-puhr BOWL): the championship game of the NFL, played between the winners of the AFC and the NFC

touchdown (TUTCH-down): a play in which the ball is brought into the other team's end zone, resulting in six points

FIND OUT MORE

IN THE LIBRARY

Bulgar, Beth and Mark Bechtel. *My First Book of Football*.
New York, NY: Time Inc. Books, 2015.

Jacobs, Greg. *The Everything Kids' Football Book, 7th Edition*.
Avon, MA: Adams Media, 2021.

Sports Illustrated Kids. *The Greatest Football Teams of All Time*.
New York, NY: Time Inc. Books, 2018.

Wyner, Zach. *Carolina Panthers*. New York, NY: AV2 Books, 2020.

ON THE WEB

Visit our website for links about the Carolina Panthers:
childsworld.com/links

Note to parents, teachers, and librarians: We routinely verify our web links to make sure they are safe and active sites. Encourage your readers to check them out!

INDEX

ABOUT THE AUTHOR

Josh Anderson has published over 50 books for children and young adults. His two boys are the greatest joys in his life. Hobbies include coaching his sons in youth basketball, no-holds-barred games of Apples to Apples, and taking long family walks. His favorite NFL team is a secret he'll never share!